Green

A history ~~...~~
Cha... ...d
and Woolwich

Acknowledgements

The authors would like to express thanks to the following people for their invaluable assistance in the production of this book:

The Rev. Canon Giles Harcourt, Vicar of St Alfege Church • Julian Watson, Greenwich Local History Library • Paul Herbert, Foreword and initial research • John Warren, Chair, Deptford Historical Association • David J. James, National Maritime Museum • Anthony Cross, Warwick Leadlay Gallery, Greenwich • Beverley Burford, Curator, Greenwich Borough Museum.

Designed by Robert J. Godley.

Published by the authors Robert J. & Celia Godley, 137 Bourne Vale, Bromley, BR2 7NY.

Printed and produced in England by Planart (Reproduction) Ltd, 9 Morocco Street, Bermondsey, London SE1 3HB.

A companion book entitled 'Southwark- a history of Bankside, Bermondsey and 'The Borough' is available from the publisher.

ISBN No. 0 9528 6441 X

Front and back cover: View of Greenwich by Canaletto, 1755.
Left: View of the Queen's House with the Old Royal Observatory in the background.

Timeless Greenwich
Foreword

The choice of Greenwich to host the millennium celebrations for Britain was the natural conclusion for a village that stands at longitude zero and is thus the first place on Earth to enter the third millennium. Greenwich became famous throughout the world as the place where east meets west; the point from which all time is calculated. It became the accepted site of the 'prime meridian' following agreement at an international conference in Washington in 1884. The decision was taken as recognition that it was from here that the definitive work had taken place for, in the words of Charles II, 'the finding out of the longitude of places for perfecting navigation and astronomy'. It was the achievements of John Flamsteed,

the first Astronomer Royal at the Royal Observatory, that led to the choice of Greenwich for the 'prime meridian'. Here, from a secluded hilltop overlooking the old Tudor palace set within the grounds of the first Royal Park, John Flamsteed was able to observe the moon and stars, undimmed by the London lights a few miles upstream. Although London has now grown to envelope Greenwich entirely, making it necessary to re-locate the Royal Observatory first to Herstmonceux Castle in Sussex and then to Cambridge, the area has changed very little. A painting by Canaletto from around 1755 depicts a majestic view from the Thames which remains entirely unchanged. Greenwich is indeed a place where time has stood still.

Contents

Before Greenwich

T he littering of Greenwich Park and Blackheath with burial mounds, at least fifty of which survived into the late 18th century, is testimony to a significant early history.

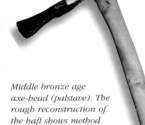

Middle bronze age axe-head (palstave). The rough reconstruction of the haft shows method of hafting.

Excavations have produced no conclusive evidence of a Bronze Age origin to any of these mounds, or of a prehistoric settlement in the area, but the probability must still remain. The dominant position of the hill above Greenwich, visible for miles in all directions, would have been an attractive option for burial during the Bronze Age.

Whatever the prehistoric activity in the area, the Romans certainly came here on several occasions.

In 1902, a Roman building was discovered on the north-eastern side of Greenwich Park. Excavations produced a significant collection of finds dating from throughout the Roman period. Perhaps the most significant of all were the rare coins from the beginning and end of the period. One coin was minted in 35 BC, whilst another came from the reign of Claudius, who conquered Britain in 43 AD.

The earliest coin is from a time when there was very little known activity in the area, and may indicate evidence of a nearby trading site along the Thames.

The coin of Claudius, meanwhile, is a rare example from the very early days of Roman London. It could even date from the time of the conquest, when the Emperor crossed the Thames on his way to Colchester, seven years before the foundation of Londinium.

Various neolithic instruments from the Greenwich area.

The Roman building was originally thought to be a villa. The artefacts, however, included a significant number of religious objects, suggesting that it was more likely to have been a temple. Further excavations in 1979 confirmed it to be a square Romano-Celtic temple, dating from around 100 AD.

Built high on the hill on the north-east side of the Park, close to a natural spring and the main road to Londinium, and in full view of the city, the temple was ideally situated; its presence also adds greater weight to the possibility that the site had a much earlier religious significance.

Excavation of the mounds on the west side in 1784 suggested that some at least dated from c. 6th century.

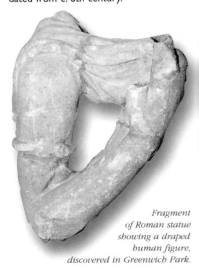

Fragment of Roman statue showing a draped human figure, discovered in Greenwich Park.

Roman floor tile, Greenwich Park. Note the dog paw print (probably wolfhound) placed before the clay had been fired.

Saxon Beginnings

Greenwich, the 'Green Port', could have been established at any time between the 7th and 9th centuries. It was during this period that the port of Lundenwic developed.

Anglo-Saxon brooch. Early Christian design as indicated by the cross at each end.

Although at some previous time the mounds had been robbed, metal military objects recovered were of such significance that there was little doubt that this site was a unique example of an Anglo-Saxon settlement.

Roman storage jar containing coins of the Emperor Trajan, 98-117 AD.

But whoever was buried here, the indications are that this area of Greenwich held a religious significance for many generations before the first major settlement developed here around the end of the Dark Ages.

Downstream from the former Roman city, the 'green site' probably developed as an agricultural, fishing and livestock centre, as well as being a natural harbour in proximity to the London-Dover road.

Edgar (944-975) granted the land by Royal Charter to the monks of St Peters Abbey, Ghent in 964 in gratitude to the formerly exiled Bishop Dunstan who held it until Henry V confiscated it in 1414.

Documents showing that Alfred the Great gave land to his daughter, Elstrudis, who then in turn passed it on to the monks in 918, have recently been exposed as forgeries, probably produced by the monks themselves.

Less than 150 years after Alfred had rid London of the Danes, they returned in force. For two or three years, the whole Danish fleet was apparently moored at Greenwich, with the soldiers encamped (although there is no evidence of this) on the high ground above - later known as Blackheath.

Roman legionnaire's skillet.

7

Male burial of the Saxon period. Note the position of the shield boss, sword in scabbard and spear head.

From here they ravaged the country, and in 1011 they took Canterbury bringing its Archbishop, Alfege, back to Greenwich as hostage. Eight months later, after a drunken feast and Alfege's refusal to allow a ransom demand to be paid, he was killed. His body was originally buried in St Paul's, but eleven years later his remains were transferred to Canterbury by road through Woolwich and Plumstead. The Church of St Alfege at Greenwich is reputed to stand on the site of his martyrdom.

Medieval Greenwich

In the Domesday Book of 1086, the manor of Greenwich belonged to Lewisham, and it indicates a small rural community with a working port and eleven mills.

Presumably standing along the Ravensbourne river, it is possible that one of these was the ancient predecessor of the former mill building that still stands

Anglo-Saxon belt fitting consisting of buckle plus three plates. 6th-7th century.

Late medieval spoon with acorn top, originally gilded. Found in River Thames.

alongside the Riverdale Centre in Lewisham. The Abbey of Ghent developed a collection of buildings down by the river, including a house known as Old Court at Ballast Quay. This building was already known as 'old' as early as the 13th century and would have been used for the manorial court.

Fragment of jug, late middle ages 1475-1525.

Throughout the the medieval period, Greenwich appears to have become an exclusive and respectable riverside market town and cosmopolitan community. Centred around the trading activity of the 'Green Port', an abundance of

Medieval buckle.

local wildlife provided delicacies such as plovers, quails, swans, teals, curlews, pheasant and peacocks to name but a few. Local peasants, however, would have been extremely poor and under-nourished, having to forage and hunt for what animals they could. Famine was not unheard of.

Medieval penambular brooch.

Wolves were a predatory local species at this time, and presented a threat to anyone venturing into woodland areas.

All artefacts shown in this chapter © Greenwich Borough Museum, Plumstead.

Revolution on Blackheath

*T*hroughout its history, the Heath has witnessed a series of significant events from rebellion and insurrection to military parades, pageants and demonstrations.

During the Peasant's Revolt of 1381, the Heath was used by Wat Tyler and Jack Straw to amass 100,000 rebels prior to their protest march on London against the new poll tax.

On 12 June, the 14 year old Richard II sailed out from his stronghold in the Tower of London in an attempt to land at Greenwich and meet the rebel leader, Wat Tyler, a Dartford blacksmith. The rebels at Greenwich, however, prevented him from landing and forced his return to London. They gave chase and occupied the Tower of London, burnt the Temple library and destroyed the Monastery of St John, Clerkenwell.

The rebellion ultimately failed, however, and Tyler was stabbed by the Lord Mayor of London, William Walworth (d. 1385).

In 1400 Henry IV greeted the Emperor of Constantinople here and forged an allegiance against the Turks.

Henry V was welcomed back from the battle of Agincourt here in 1415, but would not allow triumphalist songs and displays of nationalist fervour.

In 1450, Jack Cade also camped here with 40,000 followers as he prepared to march on London. The 'Blackheath Petition' was drafted as a list of grievances to be presented to the King.

The rebellion was savagely checked and, when Cade was brutally murdered, his supporters returned to Blackheath 'naked save their shirts' to beg the King's forgiveness.

Two years later in 1452 Henry VI's forces deftly captured and returned to London his cousin, the Duke of York, who claimed the Crown for himself.

The only King actually to battle with rebels on Blackheath was Henry VII. When 6000 Cornishmen led by Michael Joseph marched on London in 1497 to protest at taxes to finance Scottish wars, up to a third died fighting the King's army. The rest surrendered and their leaders were executed.

A small mound on Blackheath known as 'Whitefield's mount', after the Methodist preacher George Whitefield (1714-1770) who used it for delivering his open-air sermons, marks the site of gravehills containing the fatalities of Michael Joseph's abortive protest in 1497.

Other uses include 'a mount for trying mortars' recorded by John Evelyn in 1687 as "devilish murdering, mischief-doing engines called bombes, shot out of a mortar piece"

The encampment on Blackheath. Aquatint engraving by Paul Sandby 1780.

Blackheath becomes a village

Built in 1857, the church of All Saints dominates the Blackheath skyline.

*T*he heath at the top of Greenwich Park remained an inhospitable area of open land throughout most of its history.

Lying directly on the London – Dover Road, few would venture on the Heath alone without the benefit of daylight.

The 'Hundred of Blackheath' was an administrative unit made up of 100 families who held court in the open air usually at a prominent landmark; in this case Blackheath common. This '100' was a sub-division of Kent which was itself one of the 32 'Shires' which King Alfred had divided the country into.

Blackheath was renowned for its highwaymen until the end of the 18th century when it was decided to develop the area as a residential suburb to cater for the middle classes. The village evolved on the edge of the Heath as a number of large suburban town houses were constructed. The Heath itself now became a pleasant area of rural park land and, from 1857, was dominated by the new Parish Church of All Saints designed by Benjamin Ferrey. It was also in this year that the annual Fair had been banned from Greenwich leaving

only the Blackheath one. Although the bearded lady and other so-called freaks are no longer on display, the fair continues to this day.

The opening of the railway in 1849 brought Blackheath within easy reach of London. A number of schools were set up, some good and some not so good; Salem House where David Copperfield suffered is supposedly modelled on one of the worst of them.

Blackheath Proprietary School was one of the more successful institutions. Founded in 1831 and funded by shareholding proprietors who were entitled to send or nominate a boy to the school, it remained open until 1907.

A boarding school by the name of 'The School for the Sons and Orphans of Missionaries' opened in 1857, then moved to Eltham in 1912, changing its name to Eltham College. The school still exists, but does not restrict its intake to the sons of missionaries.

The Paragon, Blackheath. Designed in the late 1700's by Michael Searles, the buildings were restored after bomb damage in World War II.

Inset picture, above right: The Green Man tavern in the 1860's. Once a drill hall, assembly rooms & concert hall, Mme. Tussaud staged her travelling waxworks here in 1833.

St Michael And All Angels church. Water colour by T.H. Shepherd, c. 1829. Unusually the spire was built at the east end.

Blackheath High School for Girls was founded in 1880 and was one of the first schools in the country to offer girls a proper education.

In 1780 a large cavern was discovered beneath the Point, which is near the top of Blackheath Hill. A passage linking four large areas, including a well, still excite the imaginaton but are thought to be 15th century 'chalk-pyttes'. The caverns were used briefly in the 1850's as a venue for masked balls but were sealed in 1853.

Good quality gravel was excavated from the Heath and shipped out via Ballast Quay.

Louis XIV of France attempted to barter paving slabs in exchange for Blackheath gravel for the gardens of Versailles.

Gravel-pits dating from the 17th century were mostly filled in with rubble from World War II bomb damage. One large exception still exists but in the form of a street named Blackheath Vale.

Recreation and culture

The Green Man tavern once stood at the top of Blackheath Hill, and provided a meeting place for many years. A bus-stop which bears the same name is now all that remains.

Looking towards the Royal Naval Hospital, from the Point. from a lithograph by T. N. Baynes

Rollerskating became popular in 1870 and a rink was built on the site of the present post office for 1000 people. Half the rink was enclosed in order to provide an arena for concerts, etc. Paderewski played, and Stanley lectured on his travels in Africa. However, noise from the nearby railway meant that this was a far from ideal venue.

The Conservatoire of Music was established in 1881, and the Blackheath Art Club in 1883. The Blackheath Concert Hall opened its doors in 1895 at the top of the hill opposite Lee Road and is still a great community asset.

Prince of Wales Pond looking towards All Saints.

The Royal Blackheath Golf Club, said to have been founded in 1608 but more likely to have been in the 1740's, was, according to legend, the first golf club in Britain. It amalgamated with Eltham Golf Club in 1923.

Blackheath Rugby Club is believed to be the oldest rugby union club in the world, but some doubt exists as to the precise date of its founding, thought to be around 1862.

Cricket has been played on the Heath from about 1820 and at its peak 36 individual games would be under way simultaneously on a Saturday afternoon.

Greenwich – The First Royal Park

*I*n 1414, the manor of Greenwich reverted back to the Crown, although Henry IV may already have built a home here around a decade earlier.

Statue of William IV on the site formerly occupied by St Mary's Church, 1823-1936.

In 1415, Henry V met the Lord Mayor of London on Blackheath after returning from his victory at Agincourt.

Two years later, his brother Humphrey, Duke of Gloucester, acquired the manor when he became Prince Regent. In 1427, Humphrey demolished the old house by the river and built onto the foundations 'a faire building', to be known as Bella Court.

Six years later in 1433, Henry VI allowed him to enclose 200 acres of land, the first Royal Park in England.

A keeper was appointed for Greenwich Park in 1486, and around a hundred deer were brought here from Rayleigh Park in Essex for the King's sport. The deer were allowed to roam freely until the 1930's, when they were confined to 'The Wilderness' area. The manor house, which stood close to the present Greenwich Pier, was lavishly furnished, and became a centre of learning. The library, the most extensive in private hands, was given to Oxford University where it formed the nucleus of the Bodleian Library. After Humphrey's death in 1447, Bella Court passed to Henry VI's seventeen year old wife, Margaret of Anjou, who renamed it Pleasunce – a name which carried a similar sentiment. The young Queen made

considerable alterations to the manor, as did her successor, Elizabeth Woodville, the wife of Edward IV (and mother of the two princes murdered in the Tower). The manor was developing into a magnificent medieval palace, but no illustrations survive and the building was soon to be demolished.

Greenwich reached the pinnacle of royal approval during the reign of Henry VIII and various sporting activities such as tilting, fighting with swords and spears, archery and wrestling, took place on the flat ground at the foot of the hill.

It was at a tournament on Mayday 1536, so the story goes, that Anne Boleyn is said to have dropped her handkerchief as a signal to a lover.

Henry left early, and later that night Anne's brother and his friends were arrested and taken to the Tower. A similar fate awaited Anne the next day.

The City of London staged an elaborate mock battle for Elizabeth I in 1558, based on the Duke of Norfolk's plot. It was said to have had 'all the appearances of a regular battle except the blood'.

In 1619 James I had the park enclosed with a brick wall costing £2000.

General Wolfe. The Tait Mackenzie statue overlooking the Queens House.

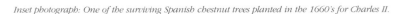

Above: Greenwich from One Tree Hill, by Vorsterman

Below: denizens of the park – a deer and a grey squirrel.

The layout of the park as it is now dates from 1662-1665 when Charles II commissioned the French landscape gardener André Le Notre to initiate a programme of re-design and tree planting, particularly in the area leading up to the Queens House. The 1660's saw the planting of many Spanish chestnut and elm trees under the supervision of Sir William Boreman.

In 1675/6 Sir Christopher Wren built the Royal Observatory on the site of Duke Humphrey's Tower, and the first Park Ranger was Charles Sackville, Earl of Dorset and Middlesex, appointed in 1690.

The park was occasionally opened to the public c. 1705 and Dr Johnson wrote his poem 'Irene' here.

When the railway came to Greenwich in 1838 so too did hordes of Londoners for their Sunday and Bank Holiday recreation. The annual Greenwich Fair was expanded to cater for this new demand but became such a nuisance that it was closed in 1857.

Greenwich Castle

When Humphrey, Duke of Gloucester built his palace by the river, he also constructed a watchtower on the hill, to defend himself and London from attack along the Thames.

Known also as Duke Humphrey's Tower, The earliest detailed illustrations appear in the 17th century, when the tower, which had never had occasion to be tested in time of war, had become an impressive residential home with one of the most splendid views in England.

Whether through decay or demolition, the castle fell into ruin but provided the foundations of Flamsteed House, in 1676.

Queen Elizabeth's Oak

Dead for over 100 years, this tree has legendary associations with Elizabeth I, Henry V and Anne Boleyn. It is certainly old enough to have been standing at that time. It fell in 1991 during heavy rain.

Above: autumn morning looking towards the south-west.

Queen Elizabeth's Oak: Used variously as a lock-up, a pavilion and an office for workmen, it once had a door, a window, a floor and a seat inside for 15 people.

The death of the boy-king

Before the boy-king Edward VI died at Greenwich Palace at the age of 15 in 1553, it is said that he was lifted up to a window for the benefit of the crowd so that he could be seen to be alive, although it was difficult to verify whether it was in fact the boy-king, or if he were indeed still alive. He was 'treated' with arsenic by a woman who afterwards vanished into history; arsenic was then a favourite way of dealing with 'problems' and was not detectable as a murder weapon until the 19th century.

The boy-king was encouraged to dis-inherit Mary and Elizabeth in favour of the youthful Lady Jane Grey; a struggle for power which saw her proclaimed Queen in 1553.

Short-lived was her reign; in August of that year Mary and Elizabeth entered London and consigned Lady Jane and her husband to the Tower.

Anarchy in the park

Following a number of incidents in London in the late 1800's, at 4.30 p.m. on 15 February, 1894 a Frenchman by the name of Bourdin was killed when an explosive device which he was carrying detonated prematurely.

On his way up the zig-zag path and apparently bound for the observatory, Bourdin lost his left hand and wrist in the explosion and suffered severe injuries to his stomach. He died later that day in the Seamen's Hospital. Scotland Yard was aware that a plot existed in London of the kind which had already caused an explosion in Paris.

This incident provided Joseph Conrad with the theme for his novel 'The Secret Agent'.

The Queen's house from Greenwich Park.

Greenwich Fair

" *Periodical breaking out, we suppose; a sort of rash; a three days' fever which cools the blood for six months afterwards.*"

A view of Greenwich Park on Whitsun Monday. A print from the European magazine, 1802.

This was Dickens' description of Greenwich Fair in his book 'Sketches by Boz'.

as Richardson's Theatre, presenting popular melodramas, pantomimes, songs and music as well as the Menageries of Wombwell and Hilton who specialised in spectacular lion and tiger taming acts.

1835 saw the introduction of the Voyage Volanté. This was the first roundabout and consisted of four boats suspended under timber beams connected to a central mast. It was powered by two men who turned it from underneath.

In Greenwich Park, games were played such as kiss-in-the-ring and running and rolling down the observatory hill; the custom was for young men to drag young girls from the top of the hill as quickly as possible 'greatly to the derangement of their mobs and bonnet-caps'. This inevitably resulted in many accidents and indeed some deaths.

It was a three day event which took place twice a year, at Easter and at Whitsun.

It grew from a small local affair prior to the 18th century, to a great attraction with the coming of the railway to Greenwich in 1836. Thousands of people came from all parts of London via train, road and river steamer to the fair, which by then had taken over most of the town.

The fair boasted such attractions

A newspaper cartoon of the period.

GAIETIES OF GREENWICH FAIR.

"Give me Holiday Hill, at Greenwich Fair, and all its rural and natural beauties, in preference to all the tight-laced formalities of High Life."

Whitebait suppers were served in the evenings at the local taverns and the celebrations went on well into the night.

There were many drinking booths in the fair; these had once been middle-class meeting places for the local young folk but with the arrival of the 19th century became places of disrepute; riots and disturbances were frequent.

By the 1850's the fair was increasing in notoriety.

The increasing disorder brought much protest from local inhabitants who demanded that the authorities close down 'this public nuisance'. The fair was eventually closed down in 1857.

Greenwich Palace

Henry VIII

Following the War of the Roses, Henry VII made Elizabeth Woodville a virtual prisoner at Bermondsey Abbey and took over the manor of Pleasunce.

The Tudor dynasty was enforced through a vigorous building programme which transformed the area close to London with a wealth of extravagant palaces both for the Crown and their loyal servants.

The palace of Greenwich was to be one of the grandest. The old buildings, recently extended and modernised, were razed to the ground. The new buildings were constructed in red brick with whitestone dressings and resembled Hampton Court, both in style and size.

The Tudor palace stretched for a hundred yards along the water's edge and was dominated by a splendid tower that extended out into the Thames and housed the King's bedchamber. The Queen's lodgings were situated on the opposite side of the main inner court, away from the river, with the orchard and Great Garden behind. Beyond was the gatehouse leading into the park on the site of the present Queen's House. At the eastern end of the river frontage stood the Chapel Royal with the Great Hall behind. A seventeenth century vaulted undercroft from the Great Hall still survives beneath the present Queen Anne building. At the far west end was the Church of the Observant Friars, founded in 1487, and probably the only building to survive the redevelopment programme.

In 1491, the future Henry VIII was born at Greenwich and baptised in the Friary Church because the Chapel Royal was

View of the 1970/71 excavations of Greenwich Palace showing the shape of the 16th century rooms and towers. This picture shows only a small part of the whole area.

The Royal Palace of 'Pleasaunce' in 1558, by Wyngaerde.

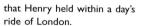

The Royal Palace of Placentia, 1560

that Henry held within a day's ride of London.

In 1516, the future Mary I, like her father, was born at Greenwich and baptised in the Friary Church. Queen Elizabeth was also born and baptised here in

Decorative leaf from Greenwich Palace.

1533 despite the differences that were developing between the King and the Friars – and it soon became her favourite palace. She wrote of Greenwich Palace that 'the house, garden and walks may compare with the most delicate in Italy'.

Greenwich was always a favourite home for the Tudor monarchs, who found here the ideal balance of majestic homelife, picturesque rural splendour and a busy port, close to the naval dockyards, and on the main route to London from where they could take advantage of the new era of commercial opportunity.

Tudor wine bottle, 1640. Excavated from the site of Greenwich Palace.

Tudor cup.

Artefacts shown on this page © Greenwich Borough Museum, Plumstead.

not yet finished. The palace soon became his favourite residence and he added to its splendour. In 1515, the jousting champion built a Tiltyard to the east of the Great Garden with an impressive gallery alongside. Around 1527, a theatre was built next to the gallery, together with a splendid Banqueting House which would have housed many of the elaborate gatherings that had formerly been held in the Great Hall. Henry also introduced an armoury to Greenwich, together with German and Italian craftsmen, to provide England with the finest home-produced armour in Europe. In 1530, the court returned to Westminster, but Greenwich still remained a firm favourite of the sixteen royal residences

Large fragment of stonework from Greenwich Palace.

Left: Royal seal of Henrietta Maria, wife of Charles I for whom the Queens House was built. Right: Royal seal of Charles I.

Tudor and Stuart Greenwich

*T**he patronage of the Tudor monarchs made Greenwich one of the most desirable residences in the London countryside.***

The restored hallway of the Queen's House.

The Queen's House from the Royal Naval College looking towards Flamsteed House.

Numerous courtiers and ambitious merchants built magnificent mansions close to the palace.

The King's chamberlain, the Earl of Worcester, was among those who built downstream of the palace. On the west side, however, were some of the grandest buildings of all. Second only to the palace was Swanne House, which stood on the site of the present market. This was the home of the Courtenay family, whose close associations with the Crown were long and prestigious. Henry Courtenay, Earl of Devon, was on the commission that deposed Catherine of Aragon and helped officiate at the trial of Ann Boleyn. A few years later, however, he was executed on Tower Hill and Swanne House passed out of the family's hands. It was finally demolished in the 19th century after becoming a brewery.

Following the death of Queen Elizabeth in 1603, Greenwich fell into decline. The departure of the Courtenay family was followed by other courtiers and advisors. The Comptons, Dudleys and Greys, who owned some of the grandest houses, all moved away. Their properties were divided up and sold to less wealthy families. Henry Howard, Earl of Northampton, was an exception. He had spent his youth in a lodge in the park and, in 1604, acquired 'Old Court' as it was formerly known, from Sir Robert Cecil. He spent £2,000 on restoring the buildings, and set up his home in Greenwich Castle. He also acquired a house on the river, formerly owned by Lord Lumley, demolished it, and built Trinity Hospital (1614) which still exists almost unchanged. James I then allowed his queen Anne of Denmark to repossess the park under the Crown, resulting in the loss of Howard's accumulated property. He left Greenwich and died soon after in London.

The Queen's House

In 1616, work began on a new home for Queen Anne. Inigo Jones, who had recently returned from Italy where he was studying the new architecture of Andrea Palladio and Vincenzo Scamozzi, decided to reproduce the style for the Queen's House. The revolutionary new style, with white cement, tall windows and ionic columns, was in stark contrast to the red brick Tudor palace. The new building was constructed on the site of the old gate house and stood over the old Deptford to Woolwich road which

The Queen's House, north front and terrace.

Henry Howard, Earl of Northampton.

1619, the old fence along the road was also replaced with a high brick wall. Plans were then drafted for closing the road, but the replacement, the present Romney Road, was not completed until 1697. The divine right of the Stuarts was eventually tested by Civil War which resulted in the beheading of Charles I. During the war, the palace was used for stabling by Cromwellian soldiers and allowed to fall into decay by the installation of 'disorderly persons'.

ran along the back. This enabled the Queen to pass to and from the park and palace without the need to cross the public highway. It is here that Sir Walter Raleigh is said to have laid his cloak over a puddle for Elizabeth I.

Anne died in 1619, and the 'House of Delights', as it soon became known, was not completed until 1635 for Henrietta Maria, the Queen of Charles I. The building was elaborately decorated and, since its restoration in 1990, remains almost exactly as it was at the time of its completion.

The attitude of the Stuarts was of the divine right to rule, and the closing of the road from where the public had been able to view the Royal Palace, typified this change in philosophy. In

> *When Charles II was restored to the throne he visited his derelict palace at Greenwich and had to break open the gates to enter.*

Although the deserted palace was thought beyond restoration, Charles admired its situation and wished to rebuild. With renewed Royal patronage, new speculators moved into the precincts close to the palace, and a number of large homes were constructed, some of which still survive. But the palace was proving too expensive for the Royal purse, and only the western wing had been completed when the project ran out of money. The palace was abandoned and the half built, half demolished site fell deeper into decay.

Greenwich Palace 1630.

The Old Royal Observatory

*I*n 1675, Charles II 'resolved to build a small observatory within Our Park at Greenwich upon the highest ground at or near the place where the castle stood'.

Flamsteed House with the Time Ball which is hoisted and then dropped at precisely 13:00 hours every day. This allowed ships on the Thames to set their chronometers exactly to Greenwich Mean Time - essential for the accurate calculation of longitude at sea.

The Galvano-Magnetic 24 hour clock which shows Greenwich Mean Time, is located on the wall of the Royal Observatory. From a 19c. woodcut.

The Royal Observatory or Flamsteed House was proposed 'in order to the finding out of the longitude of places for perfecting navigation and astronomy'.

Christopher Wren designed a building 'for the observator's habitation and a little for pompe', and managed to build it for only £520, utilising the foundations of the medieval watch-tower built by Humphrey of Gloucester, brother of Henry V (Humphrey's Tower). It is possible that one of the existing retaining walls follows the line of the old ramparts.

The Time Ball

The red Time Ball on the roof of the observatory installed in 1833, was easily visible to seamen on the River Thames so that they could check the correct time before putting to sea. This is a first essential in plotting a ship's position when away from land. The ball rises up its mast and is dropped to the bottom at 13:00 each day. Such devices used to be displayed in all the great ports of the world before radio. Now there are, of course, other ways of setting your watch to Greenwich Mean Time - by the clock outside the observatory and the Greenwich Time Signals broadcast by the BBC.

John Flamsteed 73 (1646-1719)

The First Astronomer Royal, a clergyman named John Flamsteed, began work in the Royal Observatory in 1676, setting up his instruments to study the moon and stars. His task was to find an accurate way of calculating longitude. He had a salary of only £180 per year, out of which he was expected to buy and make his own instruments. No really accurate clock had been invented at this time, without which seamen were unable to tell how far east or west they were. Ships were becoming faster, and the result was an ever increasing toll of wrecks, lost lives and enormous financial cost.

Flamsteed completed 20,000 observations in thirteen years and compiled tables of greater accuracy than anything previously known.

His achievements led eventually in 1884 to the choice of Greenwich as the 'prime meridian', longitude 0°, the division between the western and eastern hemispheres .

Unfortunately, Flamsteed's widow claimed all his instruments as her own after his death and stripped the observatory of his belongings which have never been traced. However, many instruments belonging to Flamsteed's successor, Edmond Halley (who gave his name to Halley's Comet) and other Astronomers Royal such as Bradley, Maskelyne and Airy have been preserved at Greenwich.

John Harrison 83
(1693-1776)

The need for a satisfactory method of establishing longitude at sea was becoming desperate; the increase of disasters at sea and the consequent loss of lives and valuable cargoes as epitomised by the loss of Sir Cloudisley-Shovell's fleet off the Scilly Isles in 1707 prompted the Admiralty in1714 to offer a prize of £20,000 for a solution to the problem.

A north-country clockmaker called John Harrison eventually solved the problem. Between 1730-1762 he developed a total of four mechanical timekeepers, the last of which was capable of keeping accurate time between Greenwich and Jamaica with an error of only 5 seconds (1.25° longitude) under sea-going conditions.

Harrison was awarded only £5000 prize money in 1763, and did not finally receive full payment until 1773.

This 'sea-clock' or chronometer was crucial to navigation; it showed the time at a fixed longitude on land.

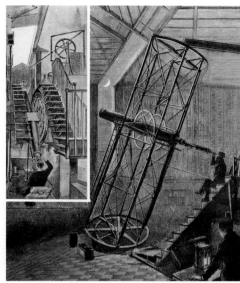

The 28" Great Equatorial Refracting Telescope of 1893. Inset: The Airy Transit Circle, which defines the meridian, longitude 0°.

Seamen calculated their longitude at sea using the sun and stars to establish local time. By comparing this with the time shown on the chronometer which was set before departure, they were able to calculate their exact east-west position at sea.

At an international conference in Washington in 1884 it was agreed that the prime meridian should run through Greenwich, in recognition of the fact that it was from here that the definitive work had taken place.

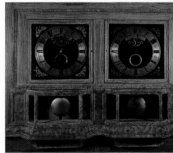

These two clocks were made by London clockmaker Thomas Tompion; their accuracy helped Flamsteed prove that the Earth rotates on its axis at an even rate.

Edmond Halley ℅
(1656-1742)

Halley succeeded Flamsteed as Astronomer Royal in 1720. The publication of his star catalogue in 1678 was the first to record stars in the southern hemisphere by the use of a telescope and led to his appointment to the Royal Society in the same year.

Continuing his work in astronomy, Halley suggested in a paper published in 1705 that three historic comets of 1531, 1607 and 1682 being so similar in their characteristics, were in fact one and the same. Correctly predicting its return in 1758, the comet has become known as Halley's comet.

Flamsteed House from the northeast, in springtime.

The South Building, containing the Planetarium.

Sir George Biddell Airy ℅
(1801-1892)

The seventh Astronomer Royal during the period 1835-1881, Airy was responsible for the re-organisation of the Royal Observatory and the installation in the Meridian Building of the 'Airy Transit Circle' which is an extremely accurate optical instrument used to define longitude 0°. Airy also developed the method for distributing Greenwich Mean Time around the world.

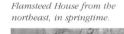

Vanbrugh's Follies

*I*n 1716, Sir John Vanbrugh succeeded Christopher Wren as Surveyor of Greenwich Hospital and decided that he needed to live nearby.

On a hill to the east of the observatory he built a fortress in a gothic style similar to the old Greenwich Castle.

This 'Gothick' folly was called Vanbrugh Castle and its theatrical style befitted a man who was also a playwright.

But Vanbrugh did not stop here. Soon he began to build other follies.

A short distance to the east of the castle was built Vanbrugh House, a massive, turreted mansion built for his brother Charles in 1722. At the end of the drive, now known as Vanbrugh Fields, was erected a grand arched gateway and along its eastern edge were built three more 'Gothick' mansions.

The buildings gained greater favour during the Victorian age when the style became popular in both private and public buildings. But between 1903 and 1910 all of the buildings were demolished apart from the Castle. This austere building eventually became a school and then the RAF Benevolent Fund School for Boys. In 1977 it was divided into four private properties.

Vanbrugh Castle. The only survivor of a number of unusual buildings built in the vicinity.

Greenwich Hospital

A group of Greenwich pensioners, early 1800's.

*I*n 1694, Christopher Wren demolished the old palace at Greenwich and started to extend the new buildings begun by Charles II.

This time, however, all ideas of a new palace had been abandoned and the buildings were to become the Royal Naval College.

The idea for a seamen's hospital followed the completion of the Chelsea Hospital for soldiers in 1692, which coincided with the great naval victory of La Hogue and the return of many wounded seamen. Queen Mary made the idea 'the darling object of her life' and Christopher Wren was again called upon to design the buildings with Nicholas Hawksmoor as his assistant. His original design included a large central domed building. Wren was determined to build a large dome in the

Greenwich Hospital, 1820.

London area, and was still being refused by the officials at St Paul's Cathedral. At Greenwich, however, he was refused not on religious grounds but on the fact that it completely obscured the riverside view from the Queen's House.

The central dome was eventually replaced by two smaller domes flanking an open vista which led up to the Queen's House. The wing built for Charles II's palace was enlarged and became the King Charles Block. The other blocks were added to produce a symmetrical plan when seen from the river – a view which inspired a painting by Canaletto and which still survives today.

The first Royal Naval Pensioners arrived in 1705, but were not used to such splendour and, in 1771, Captain Baillie spoke for many when he complained that 'Columns, colonnades and friezes ill accord with bully beef and sour beer mixed with water'. Many old wounded sea dogs complained of the excessive stairs and seemed unimpressed by

The Royal Naval College from Island Gardens, 1999.

surroundings which had pleased royalty for centuries. Despite the complaints, the number of inmates continued to rise until, in 1814, they peaked at over 2700.

West gate, Royal Naval College. The two stone globes represent the celestial and terrestrial spheres. Copper lines of latitude and longitude may still be seen.

Throughout the 19th century the numbers declined, due partly to the years of relative peace after the Battle of Waterloo and to the increase in home comforts for some which meant that they would prefer to stay with their families. In 1869 the Hospital closed due a lack of inmates; in 1873 it reopened as the Royal Naval College. The buildings were far preferable to the previous site at Portsmouth, where the Naval Academy had been established in 1733. In 1937, when the National Maritime Museum opened, the Painted Hall became the officers' mess. As Sir Charles Reilly acclaimed, this building

was 'one of the most sublime sights English architecture affords... where no careless or muddled efforts exist, where, indeed, no mean ideas can live'.

The Royal Naval College has now been adopted as part of the University of Greenwich and the Trinity College of Music.

View of Greenwich Hospital, taken from a steel engraving.

Above: The Queen Mary building.
Right: The Painted Hall where Nelson lay in state, subsequently used as the dining hall of the Royal Naval College.

The Chapel

The Chapel of St Peter and St Paul in the Queen Mary building was gutted in 1779 when fire broke out in the tailor's shop below. Completed by 1789 to the designs of James 'Athenian' Stuart, the refurbishment reflected a change in style and resulted in the Rococo interior we see today. Echoes of the naval tradition are represented by the cable patterning and the anchor within a compass rose, which are set in the marble floor.

The painting by American-born Benjamin West – 'The Preservation of St Paul after Shipwreck at Malta' sits above the altar and illustrates Acts 27 and 28.

The mouldings above are made of a synthetic material known as Coade stone, the formula for which was a secret jealously guarded by its makers.

Roundels on the pulpit and the decorated panels on the altar are of the same material.

The pairs of Corinthian pillars at either end of the Chapel appear to be marble, but are in fact made of scagliola - an amalgam of plaster and glue.

The organ was built in the 18th century by the celebrated Samuel Green and the case is Spanish mahogany.

The Royal Naval College Chapel in the Queen Mary Building, originally designed by Wren.

The Painted Hall

Sir James Thornhill was commissioned to paint the interior and began work in 1708. Amongst the various themes represented are modern and classical history, mythology and traditional symbolism; the fee for this work was £3 per square yard for the ceilings and £1 for the walls, a small sum indeed for such work. The artist depicts himself in the painting of George I and family on the end wall of the Upper Hall, his pose leaving little doubt that he would almost certainly have welcomed some additional remuneration.

Thornhill and his assistants began work in 1707 and took nineteen years to complete it at a total income of £6,685.

The west wall of the Painted Hall depicting the Royal Family, and James Thornhill himself. Painted by Thornhill's assistant, Deitrich André.

Greenwich Almshouses

Sir John Morden.

Mr. John Penn.

Trinity Hospital

*T*rinity Hospital – was built in 1614 by Henry Howard, Earl of Northampton as accommodation for 21 'retired Gentlemen of Greenwich'.

The Mercers Company are now the governors. It was rebuilt in 1812 in a 'Gothick' style, resulting in a strange, battlemented, stuccoed facade with tall chimney stacks. In the small chapel is part of the Earl's tomb which was carved by Nicholas Stone and brought from Dover Castle in 1696. The tomb has the kneeling figure of the Earl on its top. The fine stained glass window of the chapel depicts The Crucifixion, The Agony in the Garden and The Ascension and is 16th century Flemish.

Queen Elizabeth's College Almshouses are in West Greenwich and were originally founded in 1574 by the historian William Lambarde. Rebuilt in 1817 by the Drapers Company, they consist of terraces of small cottages set round a large area of lawn with a chapel in the centre.

John Penn Almshouses were built in 1884 to the memory of the brilliant engineer John Penn who ran his business in Greenwich, building and supplying marine engines to shipbuilders around the world.

Morden College

The College was founded in 1695 by Sir John Morden, a 'Turkey merchant', as a home for 'decayed Turkey merchants'. Tradition says that Sir John was a very wealthy City merchant who, wishing to retire, dispatched all of his merchandise on three of his ships and sent them on a trading voyage. However no news was heard of these ships and Morden thought himself ruined; he was reduced to earning his living working for a tradesman. Four years later, he heard of the arrival of three long-lost ships in the Thames – they were his. In gratitude, he vowed to build an almshouse for people who found themselves in poverty as he had been, as a result of misfortune.

The design of the building has been attributed to Sir Christopher Wren, but no documentary evidence exists. There is a fine chapel with a wood carving attributed to Grinling Gibbons and where Sir John, who died in 1708, is buried. His foundation is still administered by trustees – seven of the Aldermen of the City of London, and now accommodates elderly people.

St Alfege Church

Stands on ground where St Alfege (Archbishop of Canterbury from 1006) was brutally put to death by the Danish invaders on Easter Saturday, 19 April, 1012.

Having helped to lead the resistance against the Danes when Canterbury fell under siege in 1011, Alfege was eventually betrayed by an Archdeacon and taken prisoner.

He was put in chains, and taken by sea to the Danish encampment at Greenwich. A ransom of £3000 was demanded for his release.

In the knowledge that the Danes had reneged on a previous arrangement for the safety of Canterbury, and that the country had been virtually bankrupted by the Danes already, Alfege refused to allow the ransom to be paid.

The Danes, during a drunken feast began to hurl bones at Alfege; he was eventually released from his suffering by the single blow of an axe, delivered by

Thrum, a Dane whom Alfege had recently converted to Christianity.

The Building

Little is known of the original saxon church although it is the only church in Britain to bear Alfege's name. Some of these remains were most probably incorporated into the second building which was constructed during the 13th century, and later had close associations with the Tudor monarchy when the Court spent much time in Greenwich.

After a great storm in 1710, the roof of the nave collapsed, leaving the tower intact.

The present building is thought likely to be the third to stand on this site.

It was the first to be constructed under the Fifty New Churches Act of 1711. Designed by Nicholas Hawksmoor, the building was completed between 1712 and 1714; the re-casing of the tower designed by John James, was completed by 1730.

The organ console in the south-west corner is all that remains of an 18th century instrument destroyed by the bombs in

One of the surviving Corinthian capitals thought to be by the hand of Grinling Gibbons.

The royal pew has gilded carvings of a lion and (above right) a unicorn, strangely augmented with fish-tails so as to emphasize the nautical associations.

Chromo-lithograph of St Alfege Church, dedicated to the Rev. George Mathew c.1820.

The organ console.

1941. It is possible that some of the keys date from the 1552 organ reputedly used by Thomas Tallis, the 'Father of English church music'. He was buried here in 1585 and his tomb is under the chancel.

Having lost his life in the battle of Quebec, Major General James Wolfe's body was returned home and buried here in the family vault on 13 September, 1759.

General Gordon of Khartoum was baptised here in 1833, as was Edgar Wallace in 1875.

World War II (1939-45)

The Church was badly damaged by incendiary bombs in March, 1941

The Wolfe window. One of several commemorative stained glass windows.

but has been carefully restored to its former glory; a task entrusted to Sir Albert Richardson, P.R.A. The work was completed in 1953.

Some of the original wood carvings attributed to Grinling Gibbons of Deptford survived the fire and were cleaned, and re-instated.

The Nave and galleries showing part of the oval ceiling. The benefaction boards of 1710 survive, and may be seen on either side of the chancel.

The chancel showing the 'Trompe de l'oeil' painting by Sir James Thornhill. This technique involves the skillful painting of a pattern in order to create the impression of a three-dimensional design, and means 'to deceive the eye'. After the damage sustained in 1941, the work was faithfully restored by Mr. Glyn Jones. The original wrought-iron altar rails are by Jean Tijou.

Hawksmoor's oval ceiling was completely restored to his original design using oak beams 304mm square and over 7 metres in length, jointed in situ (scarfed) to produce beams of nearly 22 metres long.

This represents the largest suspended ceiling in Western Europe.

The church of St Peter, however, which stood nearby was also demolished during World War II, and the parish united with St Alfege in 1951.

Maritime Greenwich

The Dolphin Sundial by sculptor Edwin Russell marks the Queen's Silver Jubilee in 1977. The time is indicated when the gap between shadows cast by the two tails coincide with the dial plate.

*T**he maritime history of Greenwich is long and glorious and culminated in the19th century with the lying-in-state of Lord Nelson after his death at Trafalgar in 1805.***

Nelson's coffin was delivered to the Royal Naval Hospital with full naval honours.

The Painted Hall was prepared with black draperies and the public flocked to the riverside town. Greenwich was unable to cope with the strain and, on the first day, about 20,000 mourners had to be turned away. The state funeral was a magnificent display as the ceremonial barges accompanied the coffin up the Thames to St Paul's Cathedral.

The Battle of Trafalgar was commemorated in London with Trafalgar Square and Nelson's Column and at Greenwich with the Trafalgar Tavern and colonnades which connected to the Queen's

Above:
The Discovery ended her illustrious career as a prison hulk moored off Deptford.

Below:
A panorama of the River Thames. A wood engraving by Smyth, 1845.

House. The colonnades linked the old palace with new wings on either side; the complex opened in 1809 for the Royal Hospital School, a school for sailors' orphans. In 1933 the school closed and, four years later, the buildings became the National Maritime Museum.

The National Maritime Museum

Founded in 1934, the National Maritime Museum occupies the Queens House (completed1635) and the two wings on either side joined by colonnades, which were commissioned in 1807 to commemorate the Battle of Trafalgar. The Old Royal Observatory is also part of the museum.

Now the largest and most important maritime museum in the world, the museum houses over two million items including the uniform worn by Nelson when he was shot during the Battle of Trafalgar.

This forms part of the Nelson Collection which was started in 1823 in the Painted Hall (now part of the Royal Naval College).

Etching of Greenwich waterfront by Francis Dodd.

Neptune Court is a major re-development of the old Neptune Hall, providing a huge exhibition and display area enclosed under an all-glass atrium. Opened in 1999, it enables the museum to display some of its larger exhibits.

A propellor from a type 23 frigate will be displayed turning slowly. Aided by specialist lighting, it will be visible from the road outside. Paintings on display include Turner's Victory and portraits by Hogarth and Reynolds. A collection of globes said to be the finest in the world is situated in the Navigation Room.

From a 19th century chromo-lithograph depicting a fatally wounded Nelson on the deck of HMS Victory during the Battle of Trafalgar, 1805.

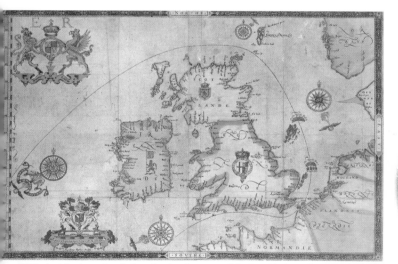

1588 chart by Augustine Ryther showing the route of the Spanish Armada. Defeated by the English fleet of 197 small ships led by Howard of Effingham and Francis Drake, only half of the original 130 ships escaped back to Spain via Scotland and Ireland.

Sir Francis Drake.

Greenwich Inns and Taverns

*T*here are a number of old established public houses
in Greenwich, some of which have long and
distinguished histories.

Above:
Wood engraving of
the Crown and
Sceptre inn, c. 1870,
one of the Tories'
preferred venues for
whitebait suppers in
the 19th century.
The Inn was
demolished in 1919.

The Yacht

Just behind the Trafalgar
Tavern stands the Yacht
(formerly the Barley
Mow) with its
impressive model yacht
sign. Rebuilt after
World War II, a tavern
may well have stood on
this site for more than 300 years. The
interior is designed after one of the
restaurants on board the old Queen
Mary, the magnificent three-funnel cruise
liner of the Cunard fleet in the 1940's
and 1950's.

The Plume of Feathers

Probably built in 1775 on the site of an
earlier public house. Rate books indicate
that the landlord occupied two buildings
which were probably demolished in
order to make way for the present one.

The Cutty Sark,
Ballast Quay.
Commands
excellent views of
the river.

Inset picture:
The Trafalgar in
May 1862, from a
steel engraving.

Cutty Sark

Originally built c.1807 when it was known as the Union. This splendid listed building, with its wooden panelling, was renamed after the famous clipper ship which is in dry dock nearby and, although it has no direct associations, the inn has a remarkable nautical ambience with excellent views across the Thames.

It is reported that the spirit of a former seaman unscrews the lids of jars and throws their contents around the pub, although this has never been witnessed during opening hours.

Trafalgar Tavern

In 1837 a small alehouse known as the George, was demolished to make way for the much grander Trafalgar Tavern. The new building was built largely to the designs of architect Joseph Kay, and was

inspired by Nelson's famous victory at the Battle of Trafalgar. The rooms were named after the crew of the HMS Victory and the balconies of the large riverside room were modelled on its stern galley.

The Trafalgar Tavern became a popular venue in the 19th century for whitebait suppers. This had begun as a basic dish served at many local inns, but it developed into a popular Greenwich pastime. By the 1830's it had become the custom for the Prime Minister and Cabinet to sail to Greenwich for a whitebait supper towards the time of the summer recess. The Trafalgar was the popular choice of the Liberals whilst the Tories would prefer the Crown and Sceptre or the Ship. Dickens visited the pub and used it as the setting for the wedding breakfast in 'Our Mutual Friend'

Ship Tavern

In 1616, the architect Inigo Jones showed his first interest in Greenwich when he bought the Blew Boar and then immediately sold it to Thomas Howard, Earl of Arundel. Jones then moved on to build the Queen's House whilst Howard moved into Greenwich Castle. The Blew Boar meanwhile passed into the hands of William Smith, the King's Sergeant-at-Arms and the first of Greenwich's entrepreneurs. Smith rebuilt the site and renamed it the Ship Tavern. The Ship was one of the three popular venues for the famous whitebait suppers.

The Trafalgar - as popular now as it was in the 19th century.

The Cutty Sark

Tam, with Nannie in pursuit.

*T*he Cutty Sark, the last surviving tea clipper ship from the golden age of sail, rests in a specially made dry dock in Greenwich. The ship's name comes from the poem 'Tam O'Shanter' by Robert Burns.

This tells the story of Tam, who riding home after an evening's heavy drinking, chances upon a churchyard where witches and warlocks are dancing. He sees one lovely young witch called Nannie, wearing what might nowadays be called a 'mini-nightie'. Burns describes it:

> *"Her cutty sark, o' Paisley harn.*
> *That while a lassie she had worn,*
> *In longitude tho' sorely scanty.*
> *It was her best and she was vauntie".*

Tam called out, 'Weel done, Cutty Sark'; on hearing him, the witches began to pursue him. Legend has it that witches cannot cross water, so a terrified Tam dashed off on his horse towards a nearby bridge and safety. However, young Nannie almost caught Tam and indeed managed to grasp and pull out the hairs from his horse's tail.

Nannie became the Cutty Sark's figurehead. One of her arms is outstretched to catch the tail of Maggie, Tam's mare.

Built in 1869 at Dumbarton on the Clyde in Scotland, she was one of a dozen clippers laid down for the China tea trade. Her owner, John Willis, spared no expense in her construction. She had main timbers of choice teak; her stem was gilded in gold leaf with exquisite carved figures running along either beam from the figure head.

The forward deckhouse provided cramped quarters for the crew.

The restored figurehead, Nannie, clutching Maggie's tail hair.

Willis was determined that she should win the tea race home from China with the first of the new season's crop of tea. However, she proved a disappointment on the China tea run, and within a few years the tea trade had passed entirely to steam ships.

The clippers were forced to turn to Australia and the wool trade. It was here that the Cutty Sark excelled. Whereas many clipper ships were unsuited to the rough weather of the southern seas, the Cutty Sark's high, wide stem rode the heavy seas with ease.

She was invincible and under her most famous captain, Captain Woodget, for ten years from 1885 made the fastest passage home with wool, once covering 3457 miles in 11 days. She became a legend in her own lifetime.

Some of the figureheads on display in the lower hold.

Soon even the wool trade passed to the steamships and in 1895 the Cutty Sark was sold to a Portuguese firm. She was employed all over the world in the following 20 years. By the 1920's all shipping was suffering in the post-war depression; the Cutty Sark could no longer be employed. She was bought by Captain W.H. Dowman and restored in 1922 as a lasting memorial to a golden age.

She came to Greenwich in 1954.

Gypsy Moth IV

Sir Francis Chichester's 54 foot long sailing ketch is in permanent dry dock beside the Cutty Sark, a symbol of a 'great English seafarer'. It was in this yacht that Sir Francis became the first man to sail single-handed round the world, from August 1966 to May 1967.

The Gypsy Moth IV is famous for covering 29,677 miles in 226 days; this averaged 131 miles per day and was the fastest solo circumnavigation of the world.

Greenwich is a fitting site for the yacht, close to where Sir Francis Drake returned from the first circumnavigation in 1581. It was at the Royal Naval College that Chichester was knighted by the Queen, using the same sword as had been used by Elizabeth I when knighting Francis Drake 400 years earlier. The Gypsy Moth IV public exhibition presents the yacht exactly as she was when sailing round the world, even down to the pots and pans in the galley, so that visitors can imagine what life was like for Sir Francis during his 226 days at sea and marvel at his courage and achievement.

Crooms Hill

A steep, winding road, reputed to be one of the oldest in London, running up from St. Alfege Church along the western boundary of Greenwich Park up to Blackheath, it contains many interesting buildings.

Red brick gazebo by Robert Hooke, 1672. Restored in 1972.

Blind fiddler outside Crowders Music Hall. It became 'The Parthenon' in 1885, then 'Barnards' and 'The Hippodrome'. Later to become Greenwich Theatre. From a photograph by Spurgeon.

From an engraving of Our Lady, Star of the Sea, Crooms Hill.

A number of houses, though much changed, survive from at least the 17th century, the oldest house being "The Grange", some of whose timbers are thought to date from the early 12th century. In the grounds of The Grange there is the building known as 'the Gazebo' which overlooks Greenwich Park; it was designed in 1672 by Robert Hooke and restored in 1972.

The Rangers House, once the home of the Earl of Chesterfield (author of 'Letters to My Son') and at that time known as Chesterfield House, was built in the late 17th century by Snape, one of three Georgian houses which stood in the avenue known as Chesterfield Walk.

It now houses the fine 'Suffolk Collection' of paintings.

Montague House, the home of Queen Caroline, was demolished in 1815. The other survivor is Macartney House, although this has been much altered and extended. It was the home of Major-General James Wolfe and it was here that his body was returned after the capture of Quebec in 1760 before burial in the family vault in St. Alfege Church.

On the other side of the road is another survivor of the same era, largely unaltered, known as 'the Manor House'.

The first Roman Catholic Church to be built in Greenwich, Church of Our Lady Star of the Sea, is found in Crooms Hill. It has attached to it, the charming tale of a Catholic woman, Mrs. North, who vowed to build a church in honour of Our Lady Star of the Sea if her two sons whose boat had capsized near Greenwich, were saved from drowning. The sons were rescued and later became priests. Canon Richard North completed the building in 1851.

Crooms Hill from Greenwich Park

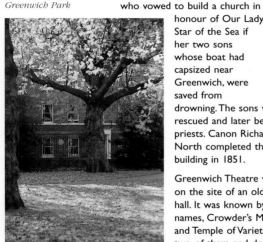

Greenwich Theatre was built on the site of an old music hall. It was known by various names, Crowder's Music Hall and Temple of Varieties being two of them and despite being rebuilt in 1885, saw a decline after the First World War, eventually becoming a cinema, 'The Greenwich Hippodrome'. This too closed in the 1950's but re-opened in 1969 as the Greenwich Theatre. Although the entrance in Crooms Hill is modern, the side

Chesterfield House, otherwise known as the Rangers House.

Macartney House, home of General Edward Wolfe from 1751, father of James Wolfe.

entrance in Nevada St. retains its 1885 facade. Sadly, the theatre has once again been closed.

No. 6 Crooms Hill – The Poet Laureate Cecil Day Lewis lived in this early 18th century house for many years until he died in 1972.

No. 26 Crooms Hill – This house has a blue plaque "Benjamin Waugh 1839-1908, founder of the NSPCC, lived here". It in fact belongs on no. 62 - a mistake made as a result of re-numbering in 1878.

The Fan Museum

No. 12 Crooms Hill accommodates the only museum of its kind in the world dedicated to the history, art and craft of fan-making. It has a collection in excess of 3000 fans dating from the 11th century. The museum building is a beautifully restored example of an 18th century town house and includes an orangery and Japanese inspired garden.

Major-General James Wolfe

***B**orn in Westerham, Kent on 2 January 1727, Wolfe was Commander of the British Army at the capture of Quebec in 1759.*

James Wolfe arrived in Greenwich when he was about twelve years old. The family moved to Macartney House, Crooms Hill in 1751.

At 14, he obtained a commission as Second Lieutenant in the Royal Marines, but transferred to the 12th Foot almost immediately after.

His courage and flair for leadership earned him a captaincy while still only 17 years old.

He took part in the suppression of the rebellion of 1745 and was present at the battles of Falkirk and Culloden. By 1750 he was Lieutenant-Colonel of the 20th regiment.

With the rank of Brigadier-General and serving under Sir Jeffrey Amhurst, Wolfe saw action against the French at Cape Breton Island, America, in 1758. The subsequent capture of Louisbourg (a fortress on the island) was largely attributed to Wolfe.

Health failing, Wolfe went home to England to recuperate, but returned to America in 1759 having been chosen by William Pitt to lead the expeditionary forces against Quebec.

In June of that year, Wolfe led a British

Force of 250 ships carrying 8,500 regular soldiers to take up positions in the St Lawrence River. However, an initial assault on the Beauport shore east of the city proved to be a costly failure.

The high jagged cliffs provided a natural defence, enabling Quebec to resist a two-month siege by land and water. Discovering a hidden path, under cover of dusk, Wolfe secretly disembarked more than 4,000 men and led them to the Plains of Abraham where, on 13 September, the French defenders led by the Marquis de Montcalm were overwhelmingly defeated in a battle lasting less than an hour.

Wolfe was wounded twice, and then fatally a third time but knowing, at least, that he had won the day. This battle in which the Marquis de Montcalm also lost his life, led to the surrender of Montreal in 1760. Canada passed then into British possession.

Major-General James Wolfe's body was returned to Macartney House before being laid to rest in St Alfege Church, Greenwich on 20 November, 1759.

A statue of Wolfe by Canadian sculptor, Tait Mackenzie, was erected by the Canadian people on 5 June 1930 overlooking Greenwich Park, and unveiled by the Marquis de Montcalm, who was a direct descendant of Wolfe's old adversary in Quebec.

The Death of Wolfe. Detail from a 1762 painting in St Alfege Church by Edward Penny, R.A.

Greenwich Foot Tunnel

***O**pened in 1902, the tunnel was built to replace the ferry which had been running since 1676 between Greenwich and the Isle of Dogs.*

It provided an essential link for workers who lived in Greenwich to reach the docks on the north side of the Thames. The tunnel was designed by Sir Alexander Binnie, and Messrs. J. Cochrane began the building work in 1899. The lifts were not opened until 1904. Costing £180,000 to build, compensation had to be paid to the watermen (ferry operators) whose trade suffered considerably when the tunnel opened. Made of cast iron segments lined with concrete, the tunnel is about 390 metres long and is faced on the inside walls with over 200,000 white glazed tiles.

It lies 16 metres below the high water mark and 10 metres below the low water mark and is 3.4 metres in diameter.

The tunnel entrance; a similar one exists on the north bank, in Island gardens

The lifts were replaced in 1992 but the original wood panelling was retained to preserve the original appearance.

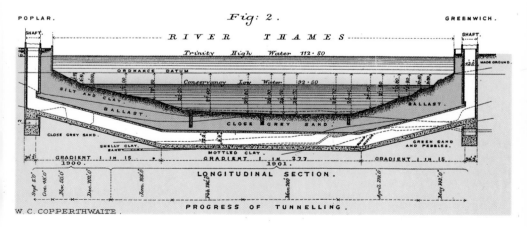

Diagram taken from the original drawings.

Greenwich Peninsula

*K*nown as Lea Ness in the fifteenth century, this area is now famous for 'The Dome'– centrepiece of a bold venture to mark the Nation's celebrations of the new millennium.

Located about a mile to the east of the town centre, by 1800 the peninsula had become known as Greenwich Marsh as it consisted mainly of marsh meadow and pasture which had never been drained.

Factories began to arrive from the mid 1820's; Youngs Rope Factory had 8 acres and produced rope, cable and canvas. It was acquired by Messrs. Enderby in 1832-33 who extended it to 14 acres for the purpose of fitting out ships for polar expeditions hunting whale and seals.

Elsewhere, a tar factory (which later became a cement works) appeared.

The manufacture of acids and alkalis made possible by the discovery of new chemical processes demanded that the toxic fumes generated be kept far away from habitation;

the peninsula thus provided an ideal location for these industries. In 1842 F. Hills manufactured sulphuric acid on the foreshore of Bugsby's Hole.

1871-1914 saw the consolidation of the peninsula as a site for chemical production, and Delta

Metals produced metal parts for armaments, lathes etc. Output increased dramatically as a result of the two World Wars.

South Metropolitan Gas Works bought 100 acres of the peninsula in 1884 for its expansion into the production of gas and associated by-products such as Coke (a smokeless fuel), Tar (for road surfaces), Sulphate of ammonia (fertiliser), Carbolic acid (insecticide), Ammonia (cleanser), Motor Benzole (lubricating oil), and Heavy oil (diesel engine lubrication), thus becoming Europe's largest gasworks.

Benzine, toluene, napthalene and sulphuric acid were also produced and used for dyes, explosives and other industrial processes.

The two World Wars saw demand for these chemicals increase, for flares, food containers and aircraft runways. Parts for guns, aircraft and tanks were produced as well as gas for local use.

The company was nationalised in 1949, and the coke ovens replaced in 1964 by reforming plants which in turn led to a decline in the by-products. North sea gas was discovered in 1968 and the gas works closed by 1978 to become a store for butane and naptha feedstocks.

After World War II a combination of government policy, ageing plant and machinery and a heavy dependence upon a relatively few major employers, all conspired against the industrial integrity of the area and resulted in a steady decline.

Fire at Enderby's Wharf, Greenwich Peninsula, 1845.

The New Millennium Experience

'The Dome' – as it has become known has been constructed on the northern most point of the peninsula on land previously occupied by British Gas.

It is 320m in diameter, 50m high (the same as Nelson's Column) and has a circumference of 1km.

The largest building of its type in the world, the area is 80,000 square metres- twice the size of the Georgia Dome in the United States.

Designed by Richard Rogers and Consulting Engineers Buro Happold, the Dome is supported by twelve 100m steel masts held by 70m of steel cable. The total cost of the project could reach £758m, funded through the National Lottery, private sponsorship and ticket revenue.

The 'New Millennium Experience' will run throughout the year 2000; at its heart will be a central plaza with a spectacular theatrical show on the theme of time, using live performers as well as the latest in multi-media technology.

Surrounding the plaza will be 14 exhibition zones which examine issues such as 'Work', 'Learn', 'Rest' and 'Play' etc.

The site will be car-free except for essential staff and access for the disabled.

At the heart of the site will be North Greenwich Station- Europe's biggest underground station capable of delivering 22,000 visitors per hour to the exhibition.

Post 2000 possible uses for the Dome include a major sports development, an education centre, a mixed leisure/entertainment facility and a conference centre.

Greenwich Peninsula and the Dome from Halstow Road.

A panorama of London looking west with the peninsula and Dome in the foreground. Picture courtesy of The New Millennium Experience Ltd.

Charlton

*O*ne of the few places in Inner London to have preserved a village atmosphere, it still has a manor house – Charlton House, said to be one of the finest examples of Jacobean architecture in the country, – a parish church, a village green and a village street.

An old public house, The Bugle Horn remains, built from two cottages and retaining some timbers from the 18th century.

Known as Cerletone in the Domesday Book, evidence of an earlier history was uncovered in 1915 that a British settlement existed on the site during the time of the Roman occupation. Present day Charlton dates from 1607 when Sir Adam Newton acquired the manor, demolished the existing building and began the construction of Charlton House. This was finished in 1612.

Money left by Newton enabled the re-building of St Luke's Church - a bequest which did much towards the development of the community.

From 1767-1923 the Maryon-Wilson family owned the manor which included the area to the east of the village, formerly known as "Hanging Wood", a popular haunt of highwaymen. Two pleasant parks, Maryon Wilson Park and Maryon Park now stand on this site.

The village green was the setting until 1816 of the famous Charlton Horn Fair, held each October until re-located to the 'Fair Field' due to the discontent of the owners.

This riotous affair reached its heyday in the 18th and 19th centuries, with thousands of people arriving dressed as kings, queens and millers with horns on their heads. The fair was suppressed in 1872.

A modern day fair is held in the grounds of Charlton House which is now a community centre and library.

1848 wood engraving of Grand Fete Champetre at Charlton House.

Woolwich

Dancing bear, Woolwich Common c. 1890. Kept in the cellar of a local pub when not performing.

Woolwich was the wealthiest of the parishes in the borough of Greenwich, largely due to its military associations.

It has a magnificent architectural heritage, seen in such buildings as the Royal Arsenal, the Dockyards and various military establishments.

Until 1889 the whole area was in Kent; in 1900 the Metropolitan Boroughs were set up, Woolwich being part of the Borough of Woolwich. It was not till 1965 that the London Borough of Greenwich was created, amalgamating Woolwich with Greenwich. It is probably best known for its Arsenal which dates from Tudor times and is the oldest and largest establishment of its kind in Britain. The first two regiments of artillery were founded in 1716 within the walls of the Arsenal, although the artillerymen later moved to the present barracks built in 1776-1802 on Woolwich Common.

Above: The Royal Arsenal, Beresford Gate 1915.

Near to the Royal Artillery Barracks on Woolwich Common, the 'Rotunda' building can be seen which houses the Royal Artillery Museum's gun collection.

The Royal Military Academy was set up in 1721; the original building of 1719 can still be seen today. However eventual lack of space forced the Academy to move to a splendid building on Woolwich Common which today is the home of the Royal Artillery Institution Museum.

The town is also the birthplace of the Dial Square F.C., better known as the Arsenal Football Club, which was founded in 1886.

The Dockyard

The Royal Dockyard was established in 1512 by Henry VIII, so that a new flagship 'The Great Harry' could be built. The dockyard saw many famous ships built; it was the scene of many royal visits and the starting point of numerous expeditions of discovery.

In the early 19th century, the yard was rebuilt and expanded to allow steam ships to be built and repaired here, but sadly it closed down in 1869, causing much unemployment in the town.

Free Ferry Service

The Woolwich Free Ferry was opened in 1889 to link the north and south banks of the Thames at Woolwich. It is still running and is maintained by Greenwich Council.

Above: The Rotunda, mid 19th century. Below: From a copper engraving of the Military Academy in 1840.

Statue of James Cook (1728-1779) at the National Maritime Museum. He made three voyages of discovery between 1768 and 1779.

One of two skull and crossbones located on the gate piers. They are known locally as 'Adam and Eve' and are thought to have been adopted by local privateers as the 'Jolly Roger'. Not intentionally macabre but meaning that beyond death lies everlasting life, the laurel leaves signify immortality.

Deptford

***S**ituated to the west of Greenwich village, Deptford's identity has suffered as a result of 20th century urbanisation and the relentless spread of London's suburbs.*

Once a small riverside village known as 'Depeford', there was indeed a 'deep ford' across the River Ravensbourne, near the point where Deptford Creek meets the River Thames.

After the invasion of 1066, Bishop Odo, half brother of William, Duke of Normandy ruthlessly took over but later fell from power. The Manor of Deptford was given to Gilbert de Maminot which passed to the Say family, and became known as Sayes Court.

The last stopping point for coaches travelling to London on the Dover Road, Lord Audley and his Cornish rebels were defeated on Deptford Bridge in 1497 with the loss of 2,000 men.

St Nicholas' church

A church has stood here since 1183 or possibly before. Richard Wyche, Vicar of Deptford in 1423, was convicted of heresy and burned at the stake in 1440. John Evelyn the diarist was once one of the church wardens. The Kentish ragstone tower is now all that remains of the original 14th/15th century building which was restored in 1956-1958 after Second World War incendiary bomb damage in 1940.

It is possible that Sir Francis Drake attended the church, perhaps to give thanks for his safe return from circumnavigating the globe, or to celebrate in 1581 the

knighthood awarded him by Queen Elizabeth on the deck of the Golden Hinde, moored a few yards away on the Thames.

Inside the church can be seen carvings by Grinling Gibbons and a few remaining stone carvings from the original Norman building.

Christopher Marlowe the playwright is reputedly buried here, having been stabbed to death in a Deptford tavern brawl by one Francis Frezer, on 1 June 1593.

A memorial plaque to Marlowe is located on the east wall of the churchyard. The precise nature of his death is still the subject of considerable debate.

The medieval tower, St Nicholas' Church. The topmost part was rebuilt in 1901

Deptford Creek, 1870's

St Paul's Church

Built by Thomas Archer in 1712-1730, it is a perfect example of the baroque style. It has giant Corinthian columns and a rich plaster ceiling and is possibly the finest example of exterior church architecture in London.

Inscriptions inside commemorate John Harrison, founder and first surgeon at the London Hospital and Dr Charles Burney, brother of Fanny Burney, the novelist.

18th Century St Paul's church, Deptford

The King's Yard

Henry VIII founded the Royal Naval Dockyard here in1512/13. Known as the King's Yard, it had two docks and three slipways upon which the vessels were built along with workshops, sheds, ropeyards

and accommodation for dockyard officials and naval officers. As the demand for ever larger vessels increased, so the decline of the King's Yard finally culminated in its closure in 1869. The last ship to be built here was the 10 gun screw corvette 'Druid' launched in 1869. To the west of the dockyard was The Royal Victoria Victualling Yard, whose biscuit manufacturing process represented the first factory assembly line in the world. Some of the naval buildings still survive along the waterfront.

Closed down in 1869, it became the Foreign Cattle Market in 1871; in order to control widespread outbreaks of cattle disease, it was thought that live animals entering the country should be unloaded and slaughtered at one place only, thereby limiting the spread of infection.

The market continued until 1914 when it was closed due to the introduction of frozen meat imports and the lack of imported live cattle.

Many famous voyages began from Deptford; Frobisher sailed in search of the North West Passage in 1576; in 1589 Sir Walter Raleigh sailed to Virginia to establish the first British colony in North America. On 3 October 1625, 80 ships sailed from here to do battle with the Spanish fleet.

Captain Cook's two ships, Resolution and Adventure were equipped here for his second voyage to the Pacific, and both Resolution and Discovery for his last in 1777. Captain George Vancouver set sail from here in 1791.

Captain William Kidd (1645-1701) legendary British privateer and pirate sailed from Deptford in his ship 'Adventure Galley', on February 27, 1696 having been commissioned by the British to defend ships of the East India Company who were being harassed by pirates in the Red Sea and the Indian Ocean. Kidd's piracy finally proved his undoing and he was hanged on 23 May 1701.

Kidd's name has since become synonymous with buried treasure and been the subject of pirate stories the world over.

Elizabeth I came to Deptford in 1581 in order to honour Francis Drake with a knighthood aboard the

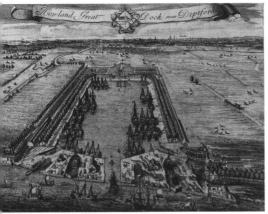

Golden Hinde, which was anchored here after his circumnavigation of the globe. The ship was hauled out of the water for repairs and people marvelled at the growth of barnacles which had flourished on the hull, for at that time it was believed that barnacles were embryo birds.

The Golden Hinde never put to sea again, but instead was converted into a banqueting house for visitors. When the ship was finally broken up, a chair was made from some of the timbers and presented to Oxford University.

John Evelyn (1620-1706)

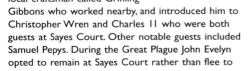

Sir John Evelyn, diarist, personality and founder member of the Royal Society (Evelyn's father introduced to England the mass production of gunpowder) moved to Sayes Court in 1652. He discovered a local craftsman called Grinling Gibbons who worked nearby, and introduced him to Christopher Wren and Charles II who were both guests at Sayes Court. Other notable guests included Samuel Pepys. During the Great Plague John Evelyn opted to remain at Sayes Court rather than flee to the apparent safety of the countryside. Evelyn left Sayes Court in 1694 to return to the family home in Wotton, Surrey.

Peter the Great stayed at Sayes Court for a time in 1698 while studying ship building at Deptford.

Grinling Gibbons (1648-1721)

Gibbons took up residence in Deptford having spent his childhood in the Netherlands where his English father had settled. By 1671 he had made his name as a wood carver and been called to decorate Charles II's new royal apartments at Windsor Castle. Commissions included Kensington Palace and Hampton Court Palace. He was appointed Master Carver in 1693.

At St Paul's Cathedral may be found many fine examples of Gibbons' craftsmanship, including choir stalls, thrones and most of the stone panels below the lower windows.

Other examples of his work may be seen at St Alfege Church, Greenwich, Blenheim Palace, St James's Church in London and a carved room in Petworth House, Sussex.

Sebastian Ziani de Ferranti (1864-1930)

Ferranti was a British electrical engineer who advocated the installation of electricity generating stations, and networks for the distribution of alternating current in England. It was eventually adopted universally in preference to direct current as proposed by Rookes Evelyn Bell.

By the age of 18 Ferranti had patented an alternator which had already been anticipated by Sir William Thomson (later Lord Kelvin); it was not only compact, but also 5 times more powerful than other machines of its size.

In 1887 while still only 23, he advanced the notion that power stations should be kept away from city centres and designed Deptford Power Station which was the largest of its time. Developing an electrical potential of 10,000 volts, this was four times more powerful than previously practical. As chief electrician of the London Electricity Supply Corporation at Deptford, he advocated the use of large-scale electricity production for heating, lighting, motor power and domestic use and correctly anticipated the use of the 'grid' system of distributing power and monitoring consumption.

Peter The Great (1672-1725)

Peter The Great was only 26 when he visited England in January, 1698 as part of his Great Embassy. This expedition was designed to acquire knowledge and study the economical and cultural life of the more technologically advanced Europeans.

Consisting of 250 compatriots and advisers, his expedition left Moscow in March, 1697 bound for Amsterdam, London and Vienna, principally to forge alliances for his war against the Turks.

England in the 17th century had established considerable seapower and shipbuilding skills; Peter wanted to study these in order to develop Russia's own navy.

King William III's refusal to provide Peter with the alliance he was looking for did little to detract from the mutual respect the two men had for each other. Staying in Deptford in order to be in close proximity to the Royal Dockyard, Peter rented Sayes Court from the diarist John Evelyn; the visit lasted for almost four months.

Sayes Court was at the time being rented out to the rowdy Vice-Admiral John Benbow, who agreed to an early departure, thus making way for Peter the Great's entourage.

Unfortunately, any relief felt by the owner upon the departure of Benbow soon gave way to horror at the damage and havoc wreaked on the property by the new tenant.

Boisterous and un-refined, Peter apparently held wheelbarrow races with Edmond Halley (of Halley's Comet fame) causing great damage to the gardens and distress to John Evelyn.

A visit to the Royal Observatory in 1698 resulted in damage to brickwork, glass, furniture and a clock made for Flamsteed by Tompion. This damage was carefully noted by Flamsteed and totalled £27-12s-6d. The Royal guest was becoming extremely expensive.

England's craftsmen had much to offer Peter; he took a great interest in, and was granted access to many skills including medicine, navigation, coinage and gun-founding.

His Great Embassy was forced to return to Moscow after 18 months due to a new revolt by the Streltsy, swhich he suppressed brutally.

Peter became a cult figure throughout Russia and Western Europe. A shrewd and courageous man, his innovative leadership enabled his country to become a great power, and his internal reforms led to progress on an unprecedented scale.

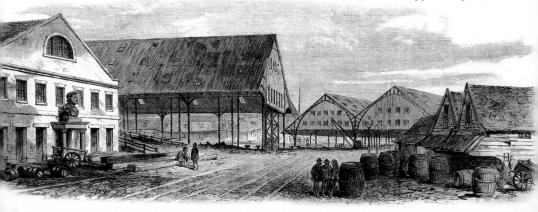

Deptford Dockyard, 1864.

London's first railway

The London and Greenwich Railway medal, 1838, struck in honour of George Walter. British Museum.

A railway line between London and Greenwich received Royal assent in 1835 and the first trains ran in 1836 between Spa Road in Bermondsey and Deptford Creek.

A considerable engineering achievement, the line was three and three-quarter miles long (6.04 km) and consisted of a viaduct with 878 arches. The track was raised in order to prevent people and livestock from wandering onto the track.

The railway had its opponents; it was not until December 1838 that the final three-quarters of a mile (about 1km) to Greenwich was completed. It was the result of a collaboration between Col. George Landmann, a retired military engineer, and George Walter, a former Marines officer and member of the Stock Exchange who was principal director of the railway company and ran it virtually single-handedly.

The Bricklayers Arms terminus in Southwark, 1844

During 1837, irregularities in connection with potential share subscribers were revealed. Whilst no legal proceedings were ever brought against him, Walter's claims for expenses in respect of the sale of his shares (which were rejected by the company), finally led to his resignation in July of that year.

Walter's plight was viewed sympathetically by sections of the press and the public who considered that being the driving force behind the project in the first place, he had been treated unfairly. A dinner was held in his honour at Deptford where he was presented with a commemorative medal struck in his honour.

Ticket for the opening of the London to Greenwich Railway, 14 December 1836.

Ghostly Greenwich

*T**he palace site at Greenwich would be unique if it was not associated with stories of ghostly apparitions.***

A photograph taken in 1966 by a clergyman, the Rev. R.W. Hardy, of the tulip staircase in the Queen's House appeared to show a shrouded figure climbing the stairs.

The photograph was confirmed to be authentic by experts at Kodak, but others remain sceptical.

Museum attendants have also reported the sounds of footsteps, but no associated sightings. Mysterious footsteps have also been heard in the Queen Anne Block of the Royal Naval College, accompanied by a 'filmy' or sinister shrouded figure.

This is thought to be the spirit of Admiral Byng who was imprisoned here in 1757 for alleged treason before being shot by firing squad on the deck of his own flagship, 'Monarque'.

The Royal Naval College has also had unconfirmed sightings of a woman dressed in Elizabethan costume, with a red wig and small crown suggesting the image of Queen Elizabeth. Away from the royal precincts, other ghostly apparitions have been sighted. An 18th century gentleman thought to be John Angerstein, has been seen at the Ship and Billet Inn, from whence he is taken by a coach drawn by four headless horses to Vanbrough Hill. More recent sightings include a leather-clad motorcyclist, thought to be the spirit of a man who was killed in 1972 seen approaching Blackwall Tunnel. Another tale tells of a motorcyclist picking up a hitch-hiker near the tunnel who promptly vanished as they emerged at the other end. The two had been talking and the hitch-hiker had given his address. When the motorcyclist visited the house he discovered that the person had in fact died some years before.

A number of apparitions around Shooters Hill include frequent sightings of a white lady at the crossroads with Well Hall Road. In 1844, a skeleton was discovered of a lady who appeared to have been savagely murdered by a blow to the back of her head; the remains were buried in the nearby churchyard and the white lady has not been seen since. Another white lady used to be seen near Morden College. This was thought to be the spirit of Annie Hawkins, a maidservant who drowned in a nearby pond after an unhappy love affair. On Hare and Billet Road, the image of a darkly dressed Victorian lady was once visible on misty autumn evenings. She was thought to be a lady who, having waited in vain for her married lover to appear, hanged herself from an elm tree. Perhaps the most celebrated apparition is from the former Public Library in St John's Park. At one time a vicarage and childhood home of Elsie Marshall, whose father became Vicar of St John's in 1874. In 1892, Elsie left for China to become a missionary, but was murdered three years later by a gang of bandits. The staff of the library have witnessed many strange incidents, such as the lights being switched on when the building is empty, and have often felt the presence of an invisible body brushing past them. This is generally thought to be the ghostly presence of Elsie returning to the place where she spent her childhood.

In recent years the figure of Inigo Jones has been seen at the foot of a bed at the Chantry in Park Vista.

Bibliography & further reading

Ylva French, *Blue Guide, London.*
Richard Baker, *Richard Baker's London.*
Nerina Shute, *London Villages.*
Tony Aldous, *The Illustrated London News Book Of London's Villages.*
Encyclopedia Britannica CD 99.
Barbara Ludlow, *Greenwich- The old photograph series.*
Franklin, Bishop, Bonner & Nutkins, *Britain in old photographs- The London Borough of Greenwich.*
Clive Aslet, *The story of Greenwich.*
Darrell Spurgeon, *Discover Greenwich.*
Reg Rigden, *The Thames on our doorstep.*
Reg Rigden, *The Romans in the Greenwich District.*
Ben Weinred and Christopher Hibbert, *The London Encyclopaedia.*
The Pitkin guide, *Cutty Sark.*
Beryl Platt, *A History of Greenwich.*
Neil Rhind, *Blackheath Village and Environs 1790-1970.*
The Friends of the National Maritime Museum, *The Maritime Yearbook No. 6.*
The Warwick Leadlay Gallery, *The Nelson Almanac.*
Dava Sobel and Wm. J.H. Andrewes, *The Illustrated Longitude.*
Helicon Publishing Ltd, *The Hutchinson Encyclopedia.*
Mary Mills, *Greenwich Marsh - The 300 years before the Dome.*

Picture credits:

© **National Maritime Museum:** *Front & back cover*, view of Greenwich, by Canaletto. *Inside front cover;* The Queens House and Old Royal Observatory. *Greenwich- the first royal park*, Greenwich from One Tree Hill, Vorsterman Johannes. *Tudor & Stuart Greenwich*, The restored hallway of the Queens House. *The Old Royal Observatory*, Tompion's clocks. *Cutty Sark*, painting of Tam pursued by Nannie.

© **Greenwich Borough Museum:** *Before Greenwich*, all illustrations. Photography; R. Godley. *Greenwich Palace*, Excavations, stonework fragment, Tudor cup, Tudor wine bottle, decorative leaf, great seal of Henrietta Maria and Royal Seal of Charles I. Photography; R. Godley.

Greenwich Local history Library: *Foreword*, Galvano-magnetic clock. *Greenwich Fair*, Gaieties of Greenwich Fair cartoon. *Major-General James Wolfe*, line drawing. *Tudor & Stuart*

Greenwich, Henry Howard, Greenwich Palace 1630. *Greenwich Peninsula*, fire at Enderby's Wharf. *London's first railway*, all illustrations. *Greenwich Foot Tunnel*, diagram from original drawings. *The Old Royal Observatory*, Flamsteed, Halley, Airy. *Deptford*, John Evelyn. *Woolwich*, Beresford Gate, The Rotunda. *Greenwich Almshouses*, John Penn, Sir John Morden. *Crooms Hill*, Blind fiddler by Spurgeon, Church of Our Lady Star of the Sea.

The New Millennium Experience Company Ltd: *Greenwich Peninsula*, Aerial view of the Peninsula and London.

Warwick Leadlay Gallery: *Revolution on Blackheath*, aquatint engraving of the encampment on Blackheath by Paul Sandby. *Maritime Greenwich*, The Discovery, Greenwich waterfront by Francis Dodd. *Greenwich Inns and Taverns*, The Trafalgar in 1862. *The Old Royal Observatory*, coloured wood engravings from the Illustrated London News of Flamsteed House, the transit circle and Great Equatorial Telescope. *Deptford*, St Pauls Church, Deptford Creek engraving, copper engraving of Howland Great dock. *Blackheath Becomes a Village*, St Michael and All Angels. *Bibliography & further reading*, The Dreadnought. *Inside back cover*, Blackheath and Greenwich by John Rocque, c. 1746 from 'Twelve Miles around London'.

Sutton Publishing Limited. Britain in old photographs – The London Borough of Greenwich, by Franklin, Bishop, Bonner and Nutkins. *Woolwich*, Dancing bear.

Laura Godley: *Old Royal Observatory*, drawing of John Harrison. All other photography by Robert Godley. Other illustrations from the authors' collection.

The Dreadnought, 104 guns. A hospital ship moored off Greenwich, from an aquatint engraving by William Collingwood-Smith c.1840